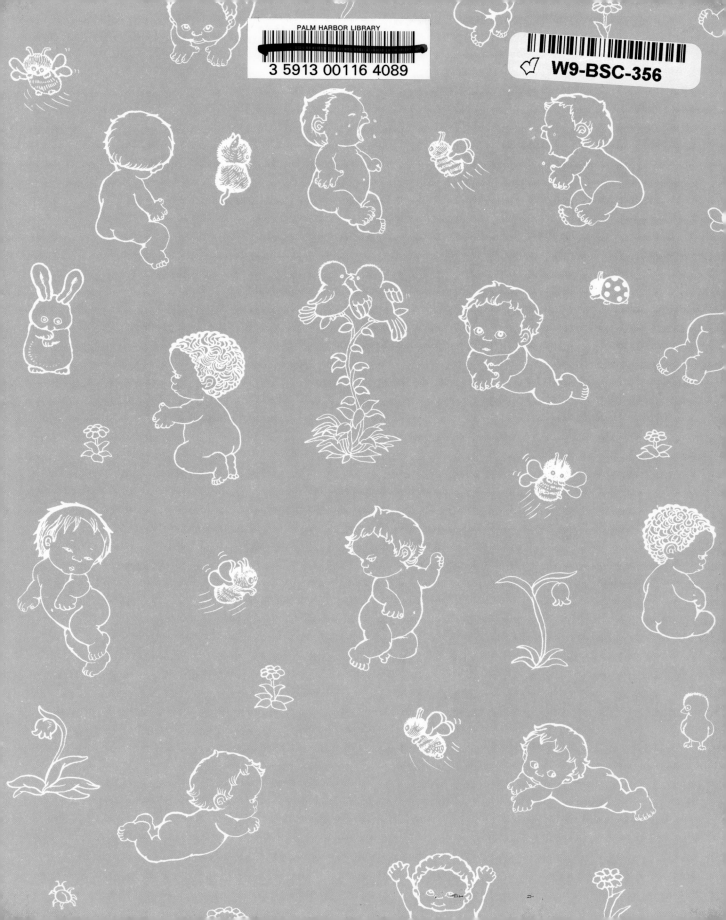

To Richard and Douglas,
who taught me
the questions
children really ask
about the facts of life

So
That's
How
I Was Born!

So That's How I Was Born!

By Robert B. Brooks, Ph.D.

Illustrated By Susan Perl

 Little Simon
Published by Simon & Schuster, New York

Text Copyright © 1983 by Robert Brooks
Illustrations Copyright © 1983 by Susan Perl.
All rights reserved
including the right
of reproduction
in whole or in part
in any form.
Published by LITTLE SIMON,
A Simon & Schuster Division of
Gulf & Western Corporation.
Simon & Schuster Building
1230 Avenue of the Americas,
New York, New York 10020.
Manufactured in the United States of America.
10 9 8 7 6 5 4 3 2 1
LITTLE SIMON and colophon are trademarks
of Simon & Schuster.

Library of Congress Cataloging in Publication Data

Brooks, Robert B.
So that's how I was born!

Summary:
When Joey's friend Lisa tells him
how babies are born,
he asks his mother and father
to tell him
how he was really born.
1. Human reproduction—Juvenile literature.
[1. Sex instruction for children.
2. Reproduction]
I. Perl, Susan, ill.   II. Title.
QP251.B7298   612'.6
81-20859
ISBN 0-671-44501-4   AACR2

Introduction

Sex education is a lifelong process. It begins with the earliest questions asked by young children about the differences between boys and girls and how babies are born, and continues into adolescence and adulthood as we seek to increase our knowledge about our own sexuality. The sensitivity and honesty with which a young child's questions and feelings are handled will be very influential in determining whether the process of sex education results in a responsible, comfortable, and accurate view of sexuality or a view dominated by distorted ideas and negative feelings such as guilt and anxiety.

So That's How I Was Born! is a resource for parents to help them to articulate and answer questions about sex frequently raised by young children. Very importantly, the book attempts to capture the many feelings that arise when children first confront the facts of life—feelings ranging from curiosity and excitement to disbelief and anxiety. In the book, Joey is portrayed as wanting answers to his questions, yet he responds to some of these answers with reservation and anxiety. As children identify with Joey, they will learn that their own thoughts and feelings about sex are not unusual, thereby making it easier for them to ask questions of their parents.

The sensitivity of Joey's parents is a critical feature of the story. His parents do not rush things and their explanations are in language that Joey can grasp, even though he is introduced to several new words. They recognize that, especially for a young child, all of the facts of life need not be taught at one time and that new information can be scary until it is better understood. They create a climate that respects Joey's feelings and encourages him to ask more questions as he is ready to do so.

Parents reading this book with their children should follow a similar course, using the contents as a catalyst to discuss sexuality at a pace determined in great part by their children. Such parental sensitivity will foster an attitude in children that has continuous value: namely, that their questions are important and the process of learning about themselves and their world can be very exciting and gratifying.

Robert B. Brooks, Ph.D.

Robert B. Brooks, PH.D.
Hall-Mercer Children's Center
of the McLean Hospital
and Harvard Medical School

"That's stupid!" shouted Joey. "I don't believe you."

"It's true," said Lisa. "My mommy and daddy told me."

"Well, your mommy and daddy are wrong!" shouted Joey even louder.

"They are not. Ask your mommy and daddy and they'll tell you!" yelled Lisa.

"I will," said Joey angrily, as he stormed into the house.

Joey's mom and dad were in the living room. "What was all that shouting about?" Joey's father asked.

"Lisa said some dumb things."

"Like what?" asked Joey's mother.

"Lisa told me how babies are born and the whole thing sounded stupid. She said her mommy and daddy told her."

"What did Lisa say?"

"She said that. . . . I don't even remember. It was dumb, anyway."

"You don't remember something that she just told you a few minutes ago?" Joey's father asked.

"No, I don't. I think I'll go up and play in my room."

"Joey, if you'd like, Mom and I could tell you how babies are born."

"Maybe later, Daddy." Joey went to his room, but stayed there only for a few minutes. He really was curious about how babies are born. Could it be that Lisa was telling him the truth?

A few minutes later, Joey came back into the living room and asked, "How was I born?"

"Would you like to tell us what Lisa said?" asked Joey's mom.

"No, I want you to tell me."

"Sure," she said, "but remember, if there is anything we say that you don't understand, please ask us."

"Okay. So how was I born?" asked Joey.

Joey's father began, "Joey, both a mommy and a daddy are needed for a baby to be born. Something called a **sperm** from a daddy joins an **egg** in a mommy, and that's how a baby starts."

"I don't understand. How does that happen? What's a sperm? Do I have a sperm?" asked Joey.

Joey's father smiled and said, "Those are all good questions. Let me try to answer them. You know the bodies of men look different from the bodies of women, just like the bodies of boys look different from the bodies of girls."

"Yeah, boys' bodies are better," said Joey.

"Who told you that?" asked Joey's mother.

"No one, I just know that they are."

SPERM   EGG

"Well, a boy's body isn't better than a girl's body and a girl's body isn't better than a boy's. They're just different from the time they're born and each special in their own way," said Joey's mother. "It's because a man's body is different from a woman's that a baby can be born."

"Really?" asked Joey.

"Really," answered Joey's father. "Remember before I said that a daddy's sperm joins a mommy's egg? Well, only a daddy has a sperm and only a mommy has an egg."

Before Joey's father could say anything else, Joey asked, "How do the sperm and the egg get together?"

"That has to do with why mommies and daddies are made differently," answered Joey's father. "One of the ways a mommy and daddy show they love one another is by hugging each other very close. In bed, they can get really close when a daddy puts his **penis** inside the special opening between a mommy's legs which is called a **vagina**. The sperm comes out of the daddy's penis and goes into the mommy's vagina, and then the sperm meets the egg and a baby starts."

Joey looked a little confused. "Really?" he asked. "That sounds weird, but that's what Lisa said too. Isn't there another way you can make a baby?"

"No, there isn't another way," Joey's mother laughed. "But what makes it sound so weird?"

"I don't know," Joey shrugged.

"That's okay, Joey. Sometimes when kids hear something for the first time, it might sound weird until they have a chance to learn more about it," Joey's mom said softly.

Joey felt a little better when his mother said this.

"Does it feel good when a mommy and daddy make a baby?" he asked.

Joey's father answered, "It feels very nice, especially since you're able to be so close to someone you love."

"Hey," Joey said in an excited voice, "maybe sometime you two can show me how you do it."

Joey's parents smiled and laughed, but Joey knew it was a nice laugh and they weren't making fun of him.

"Joey, when a mommy and daddy make love, it's private—just something for the two of them," said Joey's father.

"Well, when can I do it? When can I make a baby?"

"When you get older, Joey," said Joey's mother. "When boys and girls become teenagers, their bodies begin to grow more and more. Boys start to grow hair on their face like their fathers, and girls start to develop breasts like their mothers.

It's when they are teenagers that boys begin to have sperm and girls begin to have eggs. Then, when they're older, they're ready to become moms and dads just like you'll be able to do."

"Gee. Hey, can you see a sperm?" asked Joey.

"No, it's very small," answered Joey's dad. "You can see it only under a microscope. An egg is a little larger than a sperm, but it's still only about the size of a very small pencil dot."

"What do a sperm and an egg look like?"

"A sperm looks like a little fish or tadpole, and an egg looks like a circle," said Joey's father. "I'll draw you a picture of what they look like."

Joey looked at the picture his father had drawn. Then his father said, "When a sperm goes inside a mommy's body, it swims to meet the mommy's egg. When they join together, a baby starts to grow inside the mommy."

Joey was excited. He was learning about so many new things! He also had many more questions to ask his parents. Yet, he felt a little tired from asking all of these questions. He wanted to do something different for a while, so he said to his parents, "I feel like going out to play."

"Sure," said Joey's mother. "If you want, we can talk more a little later about how babies are born."

"Okay," said Joey, as he ran outside.

After supper, Joey took a bath, and put on his pajamas. Then he asked his parents, "How does a baby grow inside a mommy?"

Joey's father took out the picture he had drawn of a sperm and an egg and said, "Remember before we said that when a sperm and an egg get together, a baby starts to grow?"

"I remember," said Joey.

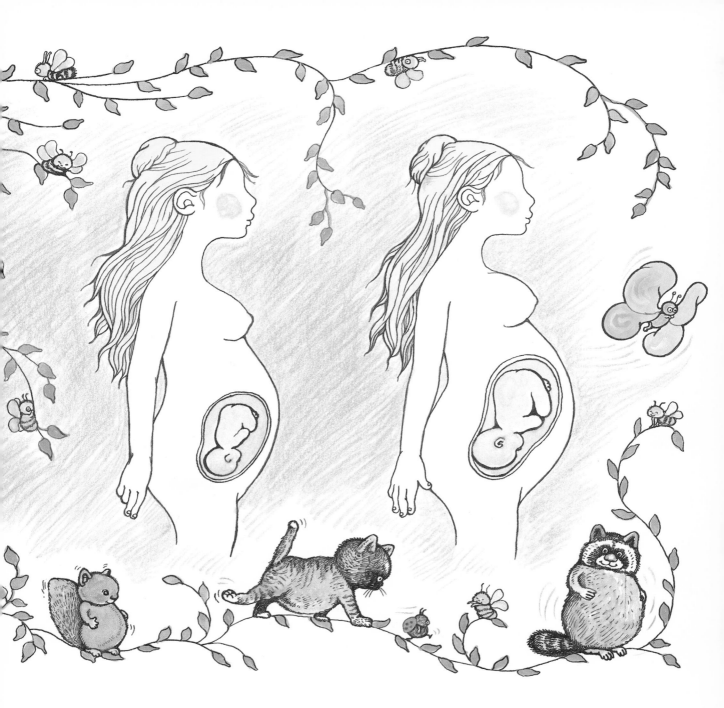

"Well, the place where a baby grows is near the mommy's stomach and it's called a **womb**," said Joey's father. "When a mommy has a baby growing inside her, we say she's **pregnant**. In the beginning, the baby is very, very small—just the size of the sperm and the egg—but it slowly grows bigger and bigger and begins to look more and more like a person."

"But, mommy, I can't remember being inside you," said Joey.

"No one can remember when they're in a mommy's womb," said Joey's mother.

"But how does a baby eat? Did I hate some of the same vegetables I hate now?"

Joey's mom smiled and said, "It's not quite like that, Joey. When I was pregnant with you, the food that I ate went to you like a drink through a tube. As a matter of fact, do you see your belly button?"

Joey picked up his pajama top and said, "Here it is."

"When you were inside me, that's where the tube was attached from your body to mine. The doctor cut the tube when you were born."

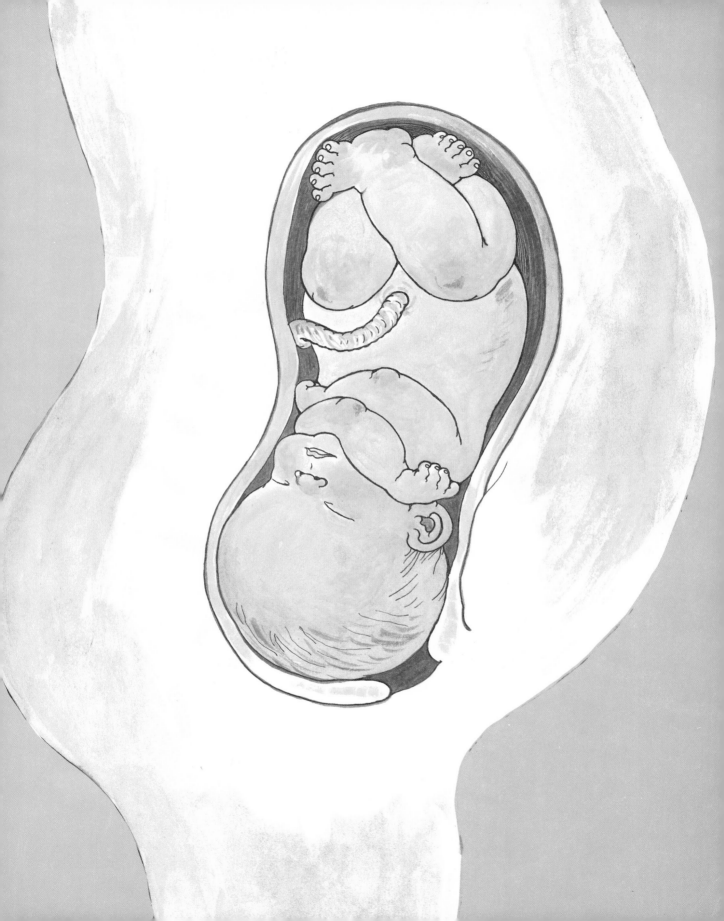

Joey stared at his belly button for a few seconds. It was hard for him to believe that when he was inside his mommy, he had gotten fed from the place where his belly button was.

"Mommy, what did you look like when you were . . . what's that word?" asked Joey.

"Pregnant," answered Joey's mother. "When a woman is pregnant, her stomach gets bigger and bigger because the baby inside her womb keeps getting bigger. Maybe Daddy can draw a picture of what a pregnant woman looks like."

Joey's father drew a picture of a woman with a baby in her womb and showed it to Joey.

"Did I feel funny inside you?" Joey asked his mother.

"You felt nice. I could feel you getting bigger every day, and I could feel you when you moved your strong arms and legs."

"Really?" Joey asked.

"Really," said Joey's mother.

Joey's father then said, "When I touched Mommy's stomach when she was pregnant with you, I could feel you moving around. I couldn't wait for you to come out so that I could see you."

Joey thought for a moment and then asked, "How does a baby know when it's time to come out?"

"That's another good question," said Joey's mother. Joey felt happy that he was asking such good questions. "When a baby has been inside a mommy's womb for about nine months, it's big enough to start to come out. The mommy begins to have what are almost like small stomachaches. Most mommies then go to the hospital to have the baby."

"Does it hurt a lot?" asked Joey.

"There is some pain," answered Joey's mother, "but it's really not that bad and it makes a mommy and daddy so happy when they see a lovely baby like you come out."

"Hey, how does a baby come out of its mommy? Is that another good question?"

Joey's mother smiled and said, "Yes, it is. When the baby is ready to come out, the mommy helps push it through that special opening between her legs that we talked about before, the opening called the vagina. The day the baby comes out is called its **birthday**."

"So that's what birthday means!" said Joey. "What happens right after the baby is born?"

"It usually cries for just a little while, and then both the baby and the mommy need some rest. After a couple of days, the daddy takes the mommy and the baby home."

Joey's mother then took out his baby book and said, "We took this picture at the hospital right after you were born."

"Did I really look like that? I look so small," said Joey.

"And look, Joey, here in your baby book is a picture of the three of us leaving the hospital. You look so cute."

Joey looked at the picture and smiled.

Joey's mother said, "When a baby comes home, the mommy and daddy take care of it, give it love, and help it to grow."

Joey's mother looked up at the clock on the wall and said, "Look how late it is. It's time for bed. Do you have any more questions to ask us before we tuck you in?"

"Not right now," answered Joey. "Maybe I'll think of more good questions tomorrow."

"Okay," said Joey's daddy. "You can always ask us whatever questions you have."

Joey's parents tucked him into bed. Joey felt happy as he was falling asleep. He had learned some wonderful facts about how babies are born. Some things still seemed a little strange, but not as strange as when he first heard them. He wasn't sure he understood everything his parents had told him, but he felt really good that they said he could ask them questions whenever he wanted.

Joey smiled sleepily because he knew that he had many more good questions to ask and many more exciting things to learn.